Door

Also by Ann Lauterbach

POEMS

Spell

Under the Sign

Or to Begin Again

Hum

If in Time: Selected Poems 1975–2000

On a Stair

And for Example

Clamor

Before Recollection

Many Times, But Then

PROSE

Saint Petersburg Notebook

The Given & The Chosen

The Night Sky: Writings on the Poetics of Experience

BOOKS WITH ARTISTS

Thripsis
(with Joe Brainard)

A Clown, Some Colors, A Doll,
Her Stories, A Song, A Moonlit Cove
(with Ellen Phelan)

How Things Bear Their Telling
(with Lucio Pozzi)

Greeks
(with Jan Groover and Bruce Boice)

Sacred Weather
(with Louisa Chase)

Door

Ann Lauterbach

PENGUIN POETS

PENGUIN BOOKS

An imprint of Penguin Random House LLC
penguinrandomhouse.com

LIBRARY OF CONGRESS CATALOGING-IN-PUBLICATION DATA
Names: Lauterbach, Ann, 1942– author.
Title: Door / Ann Lauterbach.
Description: New York : Penguin Books, [2023] | Series: Penguin poets
Identifiers: LCCN 2022030358 (print) | LCCN 2022030359 (ebook) |
ISBN 9780143137375 (paperback) | ISBN 9780593511336 (ebook)
Subjects: LCGFT: Poetry.
Classification: LCC PS3562.A844 D66 2023 (print) |
LCC PS3562.A844 (ebook) | DDC 811/.54—dc23/eng/20220701
LC record available at https://lccn.loc.gov/2022030358
LC ebook record available at https://lccn.loc.gov/2022030359

Printed in the United States of America
1st Printing

Set in GaramondMTPro
Designed by Alexis Farabaugh

To the memory of my grandmother Shaw (also Mimi),

and to the beautiful complexities she engendered—;

———*inquire, wonder, gather, respond*

Contents

We want the future to be there without ceasing to be the future.

—Simone Weil

Consciousness has no climax.

—Mina Loy

And in hollow waves of
darkness—curved and straight—
invisible, silent, something
disappeared, like a ship.

—Marina Tsvetaeva

Door

DOOR

World fills up
imperious pace

vagrant matter
into the humming

pooled at the feet
what soul went down

what inventory
mud slippage tracks

marked shells
anointed there

the ravenous real
flowering

above torsion of waves
unexpected

threshold
thrown open crossed.

BEE

Must flower. Sweet enclave. Moon.
So much for not turning up. Their inevitable,
my inevitable. Must have flowers,
pretty gold dark, never autumn.
Speak without reverence and
mind your wings. Mind later.
Must mind matter flower, dear not sun?

Then: the beautiful differences: thrall.
This plural, its gap, conscious, bald: a bloom?
Figure any of us into marginalia.
To be noted, deleted, swiped in
daily illusions of hope. O must flower.
Must allow permeable inclusions.
Blessed semblance noted, as if strong.

HAND (GIOTTO)

Over here the circle theme continues
without a clock, uncountable

and unmarked despite a pouring sound,
despite slight lesions in the rock.

A hand is waving, silently, from under
cover of cloud we said was blanketing

the sky, and so, indeed, the sky is blank
but for a reverie of reach and touch;

the ancient, fingered dark.
The word I was trying to recall is *fungible*

but it doesn't mean what I had thought,
so now I need to trade it for

another, one that means porous, means
mutable, means a shadow can pass through

unnoticed, means you turn and nothing
before comes after, nothing takes hold.

HABITAT

Do not partition or curtail the fearful crowd.
They are already stranded.
Your belts and sandals will not reach them
in their wandering distress. I myself will be
wearing a stole, with tassels.
Sometimes choices are words; sometimes they
come as tactile objects to be touched.
The contingent of insurgent migrants
moving swiftly over the stark terrain, they
have no time for these niceties, or what is
kept under our vestments, dangerously
excitable. Today in the shower I was recalling
orgasm as a layered volume of flow
so intricately woven as to be the sensed motion
of time slowly opening. Now at last it is raining.
These weathers are included as reminder
that our inner and outer
beings are breathing into the seams of the day
and that the temporal scansion
is as uninhabitable as a rainbow.
The clock, however, is full of accusations
and praise meted out
into the days; it cannot know
the barefoot figures
fleeing toward the harbor, their faces
illumined, their limbs arcing into shadow wings.
It cannot know how light dilates evening.

And dreams, what of them? Will they bleed

through, find a way to tell of our passage,

relate grass and stream,

three coyotes basking on the hill,

swirl of cloud, the hawk's high whistle,

no camera, no lamp, no held image

to capture the unpredictable path?

Enlightenments, vistas,

storied performances; everyone up close

and sweaty with desire; montage

of the nameless boy

with his entourage of lovers.

They climbed to the top of the spire

as I watched, the boy and two girls,

wearing blue shorts that flared in the wind,

and then they could not find a way down,

their bodies entangled in metal casements.

Meanwhile, branches had been collected

and arranged, stapled to a wall,

but no one had thought to find water

so they began to wither, their leaves

browned and stiff, and the woman

from the gallery wept, and tore her skirt

into ribbons that the bowerbirds took.

The bowerbirds weren't in the dream. They

are a distraction; you can look them up on

TikTok, where there are other

pranks, jokes, dances

and tricks that resemble dreams.

What happened? The secular spirit

gropes for solace and refuge.

The painter could see the scene,

depicting the sainted monk

in his habit among birds;

depicting the ravished angels

strewn across the blue wall's

firmament in a storm of grief.

These figments,

stories without witness,

rendered as material fact.

And so we stare at their silence,

its reservoir of the miraculous offered on trust.

TABLE

People gather. They
eat, drink, speak. They
are among themselves
happily. They
celebrate this or that
occasion.

          The cat
does not like
the cat door I installed.
It is not transparent.
I removed the flap. Now
the cat goes through
an open opening.

          A distant
sound, a small engine
in the sky. I recall
planes at night when
I was a child. I feared
they carried bombs.

There is something called
a transcendent table.
That is, the table does not
exist, but the idea does.
Plato's table.

I wish to be clear.
Clarity is not the same
as the literal. I object
to the literal.
What does this mean?

We had best pay
attention
to what we care about.
This is an economy of means.
To observe that life
pivots between care
and neglect.

My mother, an
alcoholic,
was cruel
when she was drunk.
She inhabits the pole
of neglect.

Care within
a paradigm of neglect
is tricky if
there is no thought of
a transcendent table.

INGREDIENTS

Went through, turned, looked back.
Is this paper? A scene? Are they kissing?
In profile, perfect, nose to lip to chin.
But not an image, not photography.
I rest my case; my case
is resting, like dough. I
went through hoping to greet you
on the dark side. Moon?
Hello, I might have called into the sky.
Hello? It might have been a question.
What is this word, *hello*? It holds
some dark components, some
poor ingredients. I speak at times
of a poem's ingredients, as if I were
making a pie. What would Paul
Hollywood make of my poem-pie?
He would say, *I'm not getting it*, the *it*
being a flavor I said I had added
but did not come through; the crust
underproved. Prue is kinder.
She compliments verisimilitude,
the sweet decorative touches
essential to taste. What shall I make
today? I am going to the market
to get some eggs, some milk.
I will see what is fresh: blueberries, rue.

FRAGMENT (STONE)

What has a soul, or pain, to do with a stone?
—Ludwig Wittgenstein

You could walk not far through the grass to the shed barefoot
restless eye landing on distance there not far you could walk
looking down at various grasses weeds clover along the way
your toes in the green the undersides of your feet the cool damp
where is significance you think as you imagine walking across
grass to the shed barefoot what counts here does anything count
on the short walk while looking down and then over then up
at the catbird in the lilac where there are now dry brown sprays
at the robin hopping in the grass over there what counts you ask
incredulous at the pace not your pace the pace of time as if
rolling downhill gathering speed wound around
itself like giant twine but invisible so not present
in the sense of seen the way you assign to the visible presence
even as what is on your mind as you walk across the grass toward
the shed is invisible names their persons hunger mistakes
the lost and the recently slaughtered because of words
believed by the hopeless lost from view tossed
into the past like a weed a rind a stone found in grass
so find solace in the particular single crow high in the dead ash
its one-note cry sky pale blue low light sliding across wires.

to Fia Backström

GARDEN

See! See! Comest thou now
quietly while the days are short
and our sleep pestered by gloom.
Come! Count sticks! Bright nature!
Sight after dark. The spot
where desire sleeps
as a gift and ceases its ancient
poison. But the serpent landed
elsewhere, blown by wind.
By then, it had no tongue
and so no way to speak.
Ribbons and wires
and silk threads were then woven—
Eve is hungry. Please conduct her
to the scene of nourishment,
sweet leaves and an apple dipped in dew.

OVATION FOR NOW

Reckless coinage, random access *once* noted furor
and air dreaming of a sibling frost
crammed into the associated hinge of cognition,

its rejected thread, mobile under the bridge,
in a hurry, gâteau, stallion, universe
swiftly traced, angled at the inky stain

ready to reimburse, flourish, spring
copied as wished metamorphoses, a film
meeting its twin along the highway's wall,

against turbulence, against an anniversary
marked for violence and the dead-end pen
writing a note to follow an exchange, the law

inconvenient, weathered, rotating into mulch
and the apparition culled from voices
raised toward the willow's ocher rain, deception

argued as an arrangement with truth, comfort
a kitchen floor and early verse spoken
although the cats and the stench and blood

blur, hurried, ancient stories in
significance, skin singed for meaning's clock
damned in its pantheon, and the hesitant few

earmarked for safety, engine of being

traced again to its end, voyeur

enchanted by gold in the cowboy hills

fast, contagious as a summit, old style,

and episodic as the wild of love

stranded there, among them, darkening

humps, additions, fortresses, in

naked versions, fit one into the other,

visitations enacted for *if* and for *then*.

HORIZON

1.

As suddenly the crimson world outfolds, flirting with
disaster along the far ridge, forgetting domestic fire,

as the arbitrary sutures hour to hour, awaiting
a sudden squall. Weather is an easy target

with its flashy abridgments, bright clouds,
as all day the meander

sticks to the fuselage of abandoned hope
and a light slings upward

toward enchantment, a noun of
great renown. Heaven, in gentle pastels,

blooms toward the outer edge of belief
and the ancient on her rickety stool, counting

ceiling cracks and filing her nails, else
collecting wood for the fire, hunched against wind.

But then the overloaded quest gave up
as other persons invaded the yard, ate all

the apples, freed the animals, tossed out
the seed, and the long haunting began without

words of advice, without summary, nothing
but wind sounding across the horizon's grin.

2.

And so the picture is crowded
with an unseen emergency

after the long session with restoration
and the problematic red scrim wounding

the body of the protagonist, whose face
we never see, whose skirts billow in

thwarting air, and whose voice, well,
her voice belongs to her breath

the way wind belongs to the trees.
Touch is another matter.

Meanwhile, sentiment accrues
in a crowded room and the clouds amass

their vagaries of gray immense
heaps, which is only time

cast across the line of sight and vanished.
Untarnished white light veers

into the restructured museum of artifacts
lost from view so the rooms

are emptied of significance, their late
hour notwithstanding, our own desire

to speak into a new atmosphere
of figures traveling up the river

anonymously; they having no names,
the stampede of missing persons

making their way across a map
that says we are going along, toward

and away, toward and away, until
we are dispersed into air's

composing its own sequence, its own litter of days.

DOOR

I don't know who lives in those houses
with pastel doors, mint green
and pale salmon. Whoever heard of a lavender
door in the middle of winter, as if
snow could dilute
alizarin crimson, saturated lapis,
deepest cobalt blue. Perhaps
they imagine a kinder welcome.
Girls not able to reach the knobs,
their pink shoes and tired crayons;
boys with missing teeth; the dog barking.
Or an elder in slippers and gown
recalling the pale sprigs of April, the scent of lilac.

AN INTERIOR

1.

I have turned my back on the mountains. Let the sun have them.

Let the sun have the river as well, I am done with it.

I am done with the sun and the mountains and the river.

Now I will stare at the spines of books.

At the spines, and the hinges, and the knobs.

The spines of books hold a chorus

singing from the dead to the living,

and from the living back to the dead.

I was about to reread *The House of Mirth*

but then recalled that we read it aloud to each other,

chapter by chapter, in bed. The sun

is setting behind my back. Behind

the knobs are secrets. I will

tell about them another time. The files are

useful; neither fully open nor shut.

I was speaking to a young man about

the ineffable. He seemed to want to find a way

to say it. I said the nature of

the ineffable is the unsayable.

The spines' address is inward and outward,

the once and never more recurring, binding

there into here, like the quick shadow of that bird.

2.

The story anticipates its assembly

under a punitive moon.

Remember me. Was that a question?

Hard to say. And don't look up.

Questions burden us

toward landscapes of old-growth trees

and the terror of the kill. Hi, it's me again,

I had a dream in which things

happened that do not and will not

in real life. I look up into

the disobedient figure of the real

and resent its sentence.

I am not a platform. The body

foresees its future, playing a certain tune

aside or beside the point

of beautiful unfolding. Belonging, yes, but

to whom or to what? I apologize. I looked up

at the eternally weeping willow.

Widow? Window? I can't tell in this dark.

COUNT

I said, *There are fewer pills than there should be.*
He said, *A robot counts them.*

My earlobe is torn. Can it be mended?
Probably, but by whom and how?

A needle and thread? A robot? Glue?
Have you noticed things in general seem torn?

Can they be mended? By what or whom?
I sometimes wish I could start again

in that other field with the magenta sky.
What to do with these ashes? What

to play when everyone is quiet and fearful?
Play some tunes from the border. Some

lyrics from the distant past of another country,
a place where no one knows the word *robot*.

The names are scented but blurry; they fall
down a mercantile ravine, awash with

meaning and the equations of logic
ripped from documents and thrown overboard.

The children are delighted; they cannot read.
They love the mighty mud and the relic tin cans.

What is that? they ask, staring at a rusty *R*.

It's the beginning of something that ended long ago.

AS IF

Credentials hover over an aftermath

spoken now   already phantom   as if a child

        ardent   surpassing   maybe adrift

on the cold architecture of ruin

               already

               under a familiar constellation of the unforgiven

                    displayed as silence

          Rat-a-tat, a-tat,

        lyrics muddied by vernacular

troubadour coiling hair around a thin finger

part portrait part song   as if   to hear

             were simple as a stone.

Or never to look out never to touch

the known viral spin

     and the body's rendition,

           revealed in perpetuity, falls

    into a lens like feathers

or snow's ragged emporium.

         And so they come forward, hurting

in their feet, breathing uneasily

into the narrative clause, into the historical imperative,

ensemble of untruths already at large

in the circulating spate of reception,

walking the streets in plaid

helping themselves to leftovers

——hungry, forgetful——

and the appearance of claustrophobic
abstraction, as if

      they have no stories to tell, no sorrow to confess,
no requitals attested by neglect,
no spoons, sweaters, shoes,
no memories to offer to the few
sitting at the bus stop in the absorption of their plans.

A doctrine of the ordinary might pivot
      to a fable to tell among strangers
      to save the incident's path from beginning to end.

As if
being remiss in the saying

always expectant

      some ingredient of the shade,
      some reckoning abridged.

DUNE APPARITION

1.

Project stalled on the path   no rescue   no easy Egypt
surmounts mourning
and romance made white again   bleached
as on a beach   thrown by percussive waves
too late to alter snail pace up the dune into tall grass
where once only worn glass was found,
transcribed across the boundaries of sea——

                      That there is no
ether-scented wind

        least of all it cannot be heard over the din

and the secret filters out into empirical fact to prove
something no one yet knows.

        The treasures of sunset are many, various and common.
As if light itself were material, folding and unfolding itself.

The suffocating bird.
The marble cylinders.
The descending mercury.

And so in all languages   storied breath   trepidation of the chorus
to be considerate of ordinary procedures   consequence brooding overhead.

The fence christened by light.

It should not be crowded; she should not cry; it did not last.

The dream dried her tongue and so the story ended,
after the vision of lovers embracing in the distance
and a blue field bending in wind.

                    There were wild

unnamed flowers bending in wind.

She would wake to the scent of salty air.
She had searched for a tune before sex.

2.

A wolf and a fox emerge from Milton's tree perched on the mantel.
Later, or further on, an Italian girl reaches, and an angel descends.
Under the bridge, a silver whale smiles eternally. It is winter there.
Later, or further on, it is spring and Eros comforts Psyche.

Distracted, she cast her eyes over to the bookcase, then out onto
a willow weeping between the branches of the maple.
Above, wires slung in duplicate, like tracks, cutting across sight lines.
A little patch of sky is visible, not a painting, not intentional.

What am I doing in these dreary quatrains? It is far too
late for quatrains, even as the word is pleasurable,

with its *qua* and its *trains*. I took a train recently, from there to here, along the river, toward evening. Toward

evening, detached again as a question. *Evening?*

DOOR

Urgency of almost   bending an arm

        around the belated   arched   made fallow

           running into the core integument   as if

       desire were potency risking an outcome

paint not quite dry

sun too hot

             still at the entrance

to step over the lacy shade's interference

so one is never speaking directly to you   you

who stepped across   whose touch once

           comforted the missing image.

THE MINES (MAGRITTE)

Time remaining.
Head clock stalks body clock
under the sign.
Camera-shy. Apple-faced.
He weareth red tie and gray suit.
Or, beached along the shore, her
un-mermaid legs and chill
tease error from surf.
This is not a fish.
Something not ready, something
else has passed beyond the day's agenda
into stray encumbrance:
an awful kiss wrapped in scarves
blown from any autumn into any dream's
hectic swirl, stymied in its wake.
Counting in place: *ta-dum, ta-dum.*

      And then?
Got ribbons? Got a shield?
We have awakened into the strut of gold
and a jay's acidic cry. The air
seems about to congeal. Maybe
it will break apart and be thrown
once again onto a necessary path.
What were we saying?
The given? A call to obey? To attest?

I'll go forever forward like a mime.

The decades, their decibels, are minor.

The parenthetical estate is single

and plural: many rooms adjacent to the hall.

Quickly the earnings vanish

and as quickly the ascertained

flops on a floral couch:

familiar distant sounds contract.

Excuse me, sir, is this your war?

Some shelter, some weeping

at the elbow of air

where the cats, the drums, the crowds,

gravel and scent, congeal.

The long rain of men keeps raining.

Have they looked down? Have you?

It's almost one, and the train

is crashing through the fireplace wall,

its long nocturnal nose bleeding.

Here it is, *toot toot* and *toot*. Long long short.

A caution to the dawn's indifference.

The north wind, were you saying;

blisters on your heels? You

ran too far in the moonlight

under the sign of Magritte

and the petty grievances of small

river towns. The trees blacken,

high hills ram a backlit sky, bottles

fill with cloud, the same clouds

the big bird sets alight, the big eye

eyes. Come October,

we were saying, things

show their naked countenance:

white chair, white torso,

great white tuba:

ta-dum ta-dum.

Dusk is a rope of sails

congealed in the entourage,

swept into a trace

no one can paint.

The inebriated air,

the starry circumference.

Rain? The same cold rain

that makes puddles into song,

men into versions of men.

The ocean is nowhere near.

So much for the gate of the given.

Listen: in the coming dark

an orange plunge and dissonant scale

tinseled, or broken, by the river.

I suspect the delirious omen. Please

cancel my offer. Too much

is at stake beyond the flowing stream.

Train again in transit, like a planet.

Don't you love it when the pale-blue line

tries to correct you and the red line

warns you to acknowledge your mistake?

It's raining again. I can hear it.
It's raining a fleet of improvised men.

But let's suppose the curse of jargon
and the ripped net of memory.
Let's agree that the villain father
is dead, the heroic father dead,
the sad mother curled in
bloody sheets, dreaming of new blades.
The assembly has disbanded; their team won.
The field where the children ran
has a tick infestation; deer, bramble, stone.
The neighbor's dog barks and barks.
Venus beats the leaves with her broken rake.
What's next? Time to ask which image
survives, which folding tent found lifted
on the winds of salvation: luck, risk, chance,
all the impatient calculations,
geist billowing toward the harbor—
black sleeves, white sails—
found photo of soldiers stationed on the beach.

for Michael Ives

TALLY

And then the dream was assessed
across a black-and-gold screen. It warned
not to look out at the veiled air, not
to recall the room
where she slept as a bear
came down the long dark hall.
This occurred in the retelling,
under the present image:
a smiling woman clutching her scarf
in front of blue mountains
and scant drifting clouds. It seemed
something had happened to give her joy.
In the dream, she was neither pardoned
nor included, trudging along the path,
dragging the pelt, as the young Icelandic man
pounded away at the partita, his fingers
routing the keys, hair agitated in wind.
As she reached the crest of the hill
she lay down on the stone cap
and began to hum, to tally the day
into the vertigo of the night's cold vengeance.

ENTANGLEMENT (DELACROIX)

The unobserved cautions its subject. Too many clicks spoil the image.

We live in the trip wire of the gregarious few. Noted.

Now calm down and say something useful to all those unnoted

others who preen for our signature, our dumb addendum.

Violence wears a pretty red bow. See? A gift of the Magi.

An endless cut and a pool of leaves scavenge grass

into glory; history's reliquary is a loose and virulent wound.

The mind is dense with color, a foldout screen not yet torn.

We were on the floor, pressing our bodies, our limbs

scalded with urgency, as if in a desert, as if under the sun.

Hunter and prey indistinguishable, lacerated, mutant.

Are you watching the spectacle? Have you fallen asleep?

The angels are suffering; their huge wings are wet.

They have not agreed to be absent although their time is up.

to Tim Clark

SYNTAX

So now, stranded now, nothing to keep:
not the potatoes churning
in boiling water, not sunset, not
all our beloveds off
while we wonder who will be next
among results without cause.
So blind to consequence, wondering
what the difference is between care and trust.
What if dollars said *In God We Care?*
Failure of the clasp, the embodied seal.

Was it spoken, the promise, its enumeration,
We this and *we this?* What
did the others say in that other history
with its distress? The world
blinking, taking account, its new
code, a nearness alert to something
that seems alive. Listen as it winds
among error without origin, deaf to response,
day collapsed from the sky, nothing
to keep. There are potatoes, and kisses,
and gatherings among the recently bereft,
last nights and sentences
begun, now suspended in the predicate's flight.

DOOR

1.

The Said closes, is closing, has closed the door.
John said, *I am the Door.* Who closed it?

And who will open it, if it is not shut
forever? This is the other question, called

from the balcony by the young Marine
in uniform, before the matches flame

and the entire arena is lit and flickering
with its own memory. Who is there?

These lights, knocks, hands,
faces, crowds, surges. *Who*

is there? The street flares again
in the mind's geography,

cascading out from the numerical
so everyone is passing, countless.

Anonymity caresses its dream
and you were there, inside me,

where no story can be told, but for
the passivity of the mute child.

2.

Is Door a wound?
Farther still, the hall is dark,

and a stranger is passing
across the threshold, entering under

rugs or blankets pulled across the small rusty
cot. She stood in the pond, her body drenched,

and the girl asked, *Don't you wash your face
before bed?* They were naked on the grass

when the iris bloomed, and the mother turned
away. There were others, another time,

perhaps by the sea, perhaps on the stairs,
where the scent of balsam and lavender pulsed.

Why be concerned? As if invited to share
a secret. The one behind the door?

There is nothing behind the door; there is only
door, a condition, a prospect, a

perception in which a gap occurs, or might
occur, and you can step into or across, you

can leap or fall, you can turn away, go back.
It's an open-and-shut choice; it's a dare.

3.

The story is always a dare. What sorrow
we have made. Earth wounded, ready to quit.

Where is the circle loved as we
went around on the great horses, riding up

down, down up, preparing? All the lit
matches; all the weak lights flickering

in the auditorium, the blasted church,
the Tree of trees. We sang along:

Yes, and how many times can a man turn his head
And pretend that he just doesn't see?

There's no one in this clearing. And the deer?
Gone from the hill, onto yesterday's

horizon. Some final animation presses down
as at the end of a film, and everyone

weeps for the lost child, for the dead doe.
The flames are lavender and gold,

licking at the charred edge of a log
as if there were no urgency.

When can I use my gun? When can I shoot?
A brute noise unsettles the open field.

4.

A drone tumbling across the sky
flagging its intent, and the unfolding

wings of a telescope. *Flap, flap,* hoarding space
only to crash into a holiday postponed

for eternity. Good we have *eternal*
so the gigabyte and its multiplication

can endure, the motherboard
go dim without consequence. I

will name my start-up
Terminal Eternal.

She got up from the bunk, damp,
and walked across the field

as the sun broke over a high ridge
and its splinters radiated outward

like transparent blades
and the air alive with atoms

of her previously intact reception,
her limbs and hair, her open mouth,

now only luminous breath,
immanent and atavistic as a spell.

5.

So those remaining
will forage for their facts

under the wood ash and the bones
of the putrid carcass decaying

in the underbrush.
The observed world will rescind

its rights to observation,
transitioned into the aperture

of an uncanny, sightless eye
careering through space

with its lidded wings
and enormous, engorged desire.

Where do we go? We dissolve,
ashes to dust, dust to an infinite

atmosphere turning its particulates
into noise, contamination, grace.

And there, there are no numbers
to calculate infinity; there is only infinity.

6.

Please do not address me as Team.
I am not a Team; I have not joined a Team.

Please do not address me as Friend.
I am not your Friend. I have never met you.

Please find another way of
counting on me other than by asking

for money. I don't understand
money. It frightens me.

Power frightens me.
I am not much good to you,

dear faceless, voiceless,
bodiless thing of the ask, dear

solicitous encounter with no one.
One hundred and six ships

backed up in the harbor and no market
for the mediocre; only

the latest, greatest will do.
I'm still waiting for

Christmas ornaments. Five cards
command, *Scratch & Win.*

7.

Forgotten discursive threshold.
Queasy opacity above, slick below,

fool's gold of the chronic impasse
between what is and what is not.

Marauding ravenous jays
wearing the uniform of the sky

plummet downward onto stones.
My father is a blue jay, dead on an attic floor.

There was no early warning, no sea breeze.
Now the future condemns

all our heralds to chiding,
indignant as crows. And the wind

thrashes at our stare, and something
leaks into the pond, some rust

found on the metal cage, the saw's ragged
edge. In winter, all our tools are silent.

8.

I know, such reading perpetuates
a stranded, stale vocabulary,

before the listing algorism
tested our mutability in exchange

for knowing the instrumental tally
of our accumulated dread,

our daily dead. The face changes. The heart
stumbles onto a clearing, as in

a painting whose surface
is a pattern rendered

as brilliant debris echoing across
the landscape, carrying our beliefs.

The layers are like a translucent cloth
flowing outward, sailing almost,

into the deep folds of a sunset,
its bloods spreading their wonder.

And this is thought, also, one
under another, waiting, colliding,

carrying all the partial images
as on a breath; phantom, unless said.

9.

Mirage, smoke and mirrors, lies.
What ails? What makes us want to stay

asleep forever, rather than awaken
to morning's fortune, as the door closes

on our skit of promise, our storied
enchantment, when we marched,

hands outstretched, singing,
onto the field, and the words spilled

into air like so many vagrant seeds
carried across, and down, and into

the river's bright agenda. Now flow coils
into an obsidian hole, and an old rake

hangs on the side of the fence
as if to entice us back into an alignment,

as if to alleviate the scheme's
reckless anomaly, its mute consent,

passed from one to another
like a masked kiss between lovers.

10.

Tenuous, the wire or thread or single line
drawn across, edge to edge,

or down to the wedge between
frame and floor, like a slip of moonlight,

an apparition where the footsteps
blur across and whatever is visible

retreats into the animate whisper
of fear. *Who is there?*

Turning away, or toward,
not answering the door, not ever

knowing who went out, came back,
went out, came back, went,

never came back. Tenuous, the sign
with the name, the false resemblance.

Waiting is a form of thought. Thought
turns away, unable to name its ancestry.

11.

Begin this imagining, pull together
whatever is unspoken, trace, enigma,

ghost plurality: the near and the other,
the mongrel dog and the brute brokers

of unspeakable acts. Is speech action?
Still the question haunting time,

just when——
Please conduct me to a place

where there are no calibrations and no outcomes.
I can hear the wind. It sounds the way

I imagine an aura might sound, hovering just
below sense, like an underpainting

never to be discovered but which is alive
with crimson, a wound, or a mouth; a smile

on the face of a stranger. The wind is louder now
but it has no word and so no origin.

How to name a sound? Call it Door.
I know what comes next; I remember this tune.

DOOR

Let's explore what words cannot.

Withers naturally, a vine.

The inauthentic pesters a sibling fear.

Target loam-studded mercy; be bewildered.

Be staggered, addicted. Speak infidelities.

She pivots. He vanishes, filmic.

Sky full of holes; bed unmade.

The accord has measured more debt.

A new word might come from an old cruelty.

Path denies misgivings, buttery hues, adjacency.

Or escape into the riddle,

a tale told once again and so too often,

signal or clue, reparation for those bloodied

by plot, trussed with shame,

hemlock boughs waving, text sent,

wires strung, pillar to post: rumor,

flaw, a *stifled, drowsy, unimpassioned grief.*

FLY

The stream collapses into a nugget   fly   irritating the air
          recently dead recalled and then
less recently dead
and then I keep thinking to write
a list *what you have missed since you left*
absurd   the days crowded with lists   since you left
and who is you you ask   as if the poem would reply in its candor
You know who you is
as if——

          Fly agitates the air   infuriating   never goes out bumps against the screen
how come everyone knows *I am not I* and what does this mean
this I among you
          and who is this you—

          The you of the late afternoon the you of birdsong
          the you of the weeds the daylilies of the far field the you of awakening at dawn
          of the sight of a bobcat   mirage of the wild
          the you of Amnesty International and the silent bikers
          the you of terror   the word that failed.
          Fly a buzzword for freedom? Hashtag
beckoning the insurmountably forgotten
and the recently mourned.
Agon of falsity enriching our fields   discontent and consent   theoretical other
          their actual grace in black lace and

discernment

the fly is berserk   the facts are misleading what did you miss?

I   lives in a corner of the world   near   yes   *They your dead.*

FABLE OF THE BARN

A green truck is passing, carrying chance
but no way to clean the windows or to

kill the stink bugs in their gray shields,
their slow march up, their endurance.

If I look away I will find some
words that don't belong to me,

stolen, borrowed, or apprehended
as the cost of an alphabet, its

acquisition, of knowledge, of song.
Singing along, I am five again,

and happy in the sand, or unhappy
watching how the boys make things

from blocks. I would like also to be
making things but not from blocks.

Maybe from paint. When I made a
painting there wasn't any time.

How to not have time? Paint.
Or wander away from

what you know into strangeness,
a sure way to cancel time or

to make time fill up and not empty out
into the missing encomiums of memory.

This adventure hurts my heart, someone
said uneasily, crossing the bridge

and entering the opening in the newly
painted barn. A season was waiting there,

with sheep, and goats, and small rodents
making the dry grass move slightly

as if in a film. The barn was there, with
the books, and papers

brittle and frail in boxes, eaten
around the edges, dry as dry grass.

We need rain, another said, *which will
cure you of the past.* The downed leaves

look bloody on the ground, I thought,
and then wondered if the poem

is a way of thinking to oneself or
thinking to others. As if you were here

as the words come, and we both wonder if
we were ever in the barn. And the light?

The light was like a kiss as the air shifted,
so there were new shadows, and the scent

of hay, and dung, and a bright turquoise
egg hidden above the broken window's sill;

and who were then looking
into the mouth where Aesop had spoken

to the leaping creatures, and went on his way
across the continents, carrying a stick

to move the grasses and to hit the stones
on his path, and to help him

across the muddy waters streaming
into the sea. Along the way he would sing

but we cannot know the tune, fast or slow,
melodic or off pitch, voice low or high: nothing

of the sound, even as it seems he could hear
what the turtle, what the hare, what the stork

said, what meanings they made,
from across the centuries into our unbelief.

UNTITLED (BICYCLE)

And then got on my bicycle through the tunnel in the snow
roiling endeavor traversing   sloped city   caressed
in search of delay
                              And the small increments troubling air
and the cool pale sky
                              wilderness errand   cauldron of hope
            lost in the fickle mirror on the windowsill   bird
                        casting about for seed   body unencumbered
                              soul flight   a vocabulary of
            simple delusion
                  everything on hold but for the ditch.

Time worn through   mere fabric or scrim   girl on her bike uphill
            boy under the covers   the mouth of the dream open
                  through snow   a wilderness errand recalling
                  the nameless door and the cold handlebars and the trek

upstream and the contagion of fear
                                          body still on its journey
                  silent mud in the aftermath of rain.

And the perpetual alliance of love grown from seed
the far field's   contagion inhaled across boundaries—

Virgil is on the floor. Euripides on the floor.
No one could direct me to the room even as I was wearing
thin blue plastic gloves out of which a bug

crawled and sat on my finger as if it were a rock.

Like a god, I crushed it.

NIGHTS IN THE ASYNTACTICAL WORLD

1.

Sparked enemy cluster   radiant ball

applied blue fuel

cast nearly to sated arrangements   pooled

clamor for arrival near the   other

ocean   claustrophobia

washed out cauldron miles

uploaded for the licensed opera

begun under weight of the never seen

between atmospheric ages

apparitions once annealed

into the pre-logistical curve

mountain arc trail fate

suffered among   skip adventure   atoms

a nation's flames habitat   scorched   reflected

the instant

arrival as of final last   star

apogee flown now   detained as signal

upheld local   celebrants

hazed adventure

vernacular gun   heavy   struck

leveraged

by knowing the turn's yield   glad pearl

path drawn not soon   not   underway.

2.

Crave earth gone moody sold under wraps face obscure murder
dressed meekly assuage reason tech trimmings coil drainage
acquisition procedural blast-studded trial crested
flow after auction blockage oily vision's gaping retrieval.

After lens doubt formidable recess pulse drowning matter
sign of curtain trigger namesake token permanent closure
aching for rhythm literal extension dusted power permission
came lately drawn callow predicate Latin tarnished flickering ball.

Fictive recursive hold finger after jazz after halo after
market verbatim shallow encounter crisis adage to dwell
skeptical bondage filled fact acres wall needy repair
the sutured redemption the dissonant tide tower mirror.

Happy for touch the hill the declension of habit poison
aged poison reason answers redundant crisis of mind.

3.

Slowed to an apparatus say of speech frequented
in the collect of sighs urns signal aspiration

not close to sleep now gathering torn burdened
close to awakened trivial rugs glass trivial lyric

architectural tonic foreseeable trains as immobile
sky clad in broken gloomy barricades for birds

titled as song reaching pitches pitch as tonal degrees
married among fallen disputations of a silent partner's

woes. Cat wants food. Kids want more. Mundane
ballet of ordinary refusals at the kitchen's narrative

gloss. Heart's nightly refrains collect standard
feather dressed radical erasures clausal yet kissed

as by art. Care marvels. Sleeping crass ending totals
under tarp hoped encounter cancels sex.

Desertion hopscotch plenitude graffiti
across migrant goals logged smoked down bridge

not to look dressed numbers under stark
killer mobs fortune music gets traded on show

forget it went trolled forget trails underfoot
weather delay and the yellowing willow aflame

drastic choice undo the fire settled claim
resting on knowledge and damaged continue

damned then halt ask them stop as on an altar
as on a stoop pink bat leaf pink ball underfoot

had hidden name had filtered passage
striving to enter to climb the mosaic render the icon

a poppy or rose a title or a blessing water

a spoken allowance for margins to braid an infinite reel.

4.

To address scandal nerve vibration culled fingered

blast moon roams doom grass natural conundrum paint

slander high vigil forest over frontispiece you vanquished

antics slow mosquito wintered playtime exaggerated now

a paw stretched hair loose array feminine secreted thus

abundant seek bliss say kindness measured enrollment

among ill met speaking strangers' unseen halo

these amendments culled to be spoken the stories tell

and meet still carry emblems order traced conundrum

on shelves interior volume and acres persist

allowance repeated enclosure respite trail footprints

signed fox itinerant child hears cry comfort this note

raising better often pulse star visible anthem

coterminous near fables belonging to none still

mute vehicle fugue mainstay rode slippery gamut

futurity solved musical palace domed receptacle torn

further as if when these evasions wrist ascendant

figured as classical ambit monks among thieves

again softly appended grace further structured mode

terrible arch hollow with dolls meager at best turgid

also blown arms raised hello formerly stranded gold

silhouette against trouble seductive aggression marvel

holy in plastic garbled yet forsaken for whom knowledge

give travelers their punitive roam at twilight this time

feathers united float glue dangle to obstruct harmonic

rendered as marvel orange dust ready not sooner

the vagary ends. Would more appreciate a must for all

to listen partition to regulate form a ring's shambles tonight.

UNTITLED (CROW)

Raven vanquished, or
ask the dead sister how are things
in the blameless, in the hovering,

called by another name,
called by a slovenly practice,
flying black. We

caused this. We, assembled,
caused this perfidy and gloss,
this dread. Down the street

massive sound, dear sister,
loud blade dismantling
a maple, limb by limb, is

not a metaphor although
could become.
The dismantled limbs,

a cry from above, staggered
across the bloom of no time,
which you might have overheard

through the flames heating our
world, which we, assembled, caused.

ELEGY IN JANUARY

You have missed so much
have been absent so long there is no way

to list the things you have missed no way as if
describing the sunset day after day would begin

but it, ephemeral, indistinguishable, even
when there are storms, as now, thunder moving

across the upper reaches, rain descending, the
sky flash lit and then, as now, quiet, the rain

delicate, falling from the maple leaves
as the thunder moves off,

you missed this storm as I will
miss but not the fear that rides up, not

the reckoning, which our mother loved, inner
storm met, downpouring, you did not

miss those but this and the pale afterlight.
The pale afterlight I recall on the train to Washington,

thinking you would not see the spring then
or ever, not cherry blossoms, not rhododendrons,

not tulips as we approached the city, which now
has seen a storm rupture in broad winter sunlight.

ALARM

The girl is an alarm. Her lust is always articulate.

                                        —Lisa Robertson

Come here little girl
little green-eyed
                greedy girl
            come along the sacred dial   its fortune
                        wheeling across a childless night   come
out from the damaged sphere of gods   do not look   they
are contained in marble   they are
not familiar with your pain   have no room
for choice

                            as if to stagger the vocabulary   love into increments
as if to not dip down into the vulgate of dreams   *he he he*
touched *he* left   *he he*   smiled along the coastal lace
the bloodied sheets   ships ship   all the muscular boys all cause
shackled from that entourage to this   greedy girl   drowned
in the ancestral atmosphere   pulleys   landings   rocks   preachers   goods
                    bloodied lace roiling along the coast   the plantation shed
find the goodness find the burning brand fire seared   and sing
into the wasted lingo of hope o   greedy girl.

Chimes aggregate repetitive   coal sand pebble cloud crop
and the sad petals   white rose   brown on the floor   white rose
furiously   pure down to earth   greedy girl   comes down into earth
brown petals   this indictment   crime   the plural indictment
the force of a name   greedy girl   with your silver shoes your torn slip.

Sniff the broken lobe, the soiled petals. Walk swiftly across the parched field.
Stay in the refrain of never no more

      walk swiftly   carry your dull weapons greedy girl your rusty blade

          your parcel of seed. Recall

    the stairwell and the toppled house   recall Jonah

        the flight out of Egypt   recall the rivers of Babylon

          recall smoke and the blistering flesh

        the scent of fear   greedy girl the towering flames

          rising over the circumference the blue peninsula

some psalm   some song   some dance   this way   some path

         come along

   greedy girl across the burning meadow approaching the roofs rising above

    the stony earth

       plural rage   greedy girl   plural tears.

REVISION

Others *are* happy: *it's gonna be a bright, bright,*
sunshiny day! And who exactly are your friends?
And who—
a darkening answer asks ugly questions.
Looking into the fading light's
hymn to forgetfulness—syllabic count arcing
toward a feared encounter with
the real. Where? Over there, across the river,
among Pilgrim ancestors and their crimes.

COINCIDENCE OF THE HOE

Triangles, that old trope, thee and me
and her, or she and thee and me, or
they. Not sure how to triangulate *they*,
though happy for their plural.
Plurals and triangles are possibly
not congruent; this has to do with space,
perhaps, as well as versions
not so easily assigned to
geometry. Maybe shape-shifters; maybe
a great morphological charm,
unsteady and unpredictable, in
which mother and father and child
merge into another field of assent,
so you are not my rescue and I am not
their victim, and neither of us has a clue
how the plural will next appear.

DOOR

And then we fell into the hands
of a person who had lost her keys, so
we were stranded
at the airport without a note, or an address,
free, ready to run
into halls dense with slogans and slots,
and the cold blue light of a fabricated dawn.
This image must be fictive, none of us is
traveling with another,
we are each on our own,
wearing the spotted pants of a clown
and listening to our own music, note
by note, not humming along
for fear of disturbing you, sitting on
that soiled bench in front of a door.
What is this story? Legend has it
she traveled alone so that she could see
everything more clearly. What she saw
she turned into something to say, and
what she heard she turned into
a different music, unaccompanied
by the crowd now racing into the screen.

ETHOS

Someone must have predicted this, some Jeremiah
not believing in the new renewals of the new,
the ineluctable flower. Someone must have seen this
coming, someone familiar with if-then relations.
Someone looking down, back hunched with bending,
following the dark ground, following the track, who
saw the tunnel and water sluicing through, the fires
leaping, ravenous, melting copper pans, killing the dog.

In high school, a teacher introduced the idea of an ethos.
It was difficult to comprehend. What was an
ethos? Our teacher, Mr. Cooper, spent some time
defining ethos. We were reading *The Odyssey*,
so I suppose he was talking about ancient Greece,
its ethos. Are we at the end of an ethos? I am
not but we are. But if *we* includes me, then I am.

A young man, Joe, is working for Verizon.
He is almost twenty-three, he tells me. He and I are
waiting for the service phone to pick up
so he can change my forgotten Verizon
passcode. It is very hot outside.
We are on hold. He doesn't appear eager
to engage in conversation; he
must think I am an old woman who forgets
more than a passcode. He has dark hair
and dark eyes and is very thin and not tall.

Is attention a form of retention, of preservation?
Is this why numbers as facts matter?
Anyway, waiting as we were, on a hot July day,
we begin a conversation. He tells me he had been
enlisted, and had served in Kuwait and Iraq.
I don't recall now why he told me; perhaps because
I had asked about working for Verizon.

There is a painting in the Alice Neel exhibition
at the Met, called *Fuller Brush Man.* I
did not read the wall card's description
because I find them mostly patronizing.
In any case, I wondered how many
of the crowded melee of viewers knew
what a Fuller Brush man is, and recalled
that a man came to the door with a suitcase
full of brushes for sale. *Mom,* we called,
the Fuller Brush man is here!

Simone Weil talks about attention.
To what should we attend?
Attention is a form of response, not just
perception. If you attend, you respond;
otherwise you are in an aesthetic morality,
pleased with yourself for seeing. We see and
we say, but what do we do? This question
sits, like a huge stone on top of modernity's ethos.

AND THEN

What does it take to persuade otherwise? We
do not listen; we do not reason. What
does it mean to listen to reason
in an unreasonable
time? Searching. Nothing is forthcoming
to tell how to persuade otherwise. They
gather in mourning, dumbfounded. Boys, guns.
Boy in charge of boys, guns. Boy without joy,
humor, kindness. Boy unreasonable, on fire
with power, the power of fire, transfigured.

Witness blood and the immobile emoji
heart, trespassing. Beloveds flee, one by one,
into the dry ghost fields
and the immaculate dawn
arrayed behind the stark arms of the unleafed tree.
The catbird has given up its joyful mimicry, now only
scolds, withholding song, perhaps never known—
what does it know, the catbird? Color of storm.

SONG (UKRAINE)

These tears are Wiki-leaks in the cloister
moister than God's more numerous than fleas
teased onto pillow slips
lips parted with sorrow.
Who are we to doubt
shout tirades belonging to the many
plenty-to-do-or-not-to-do lists
fists and other bodily parts
darts through the streets knotted
plotted in the darkest season
reason enough for hell's
bells to celebrate the fledgling human
numen or trace or history's fact.
Lack and loss, speed bumps
jumps, bombs, flames, and tidings of more
stored as an old sign where it pivots:
give it a name, time will tell: peace
leased unto the spirit, yours, theirs, ours. Or else.

THE BELATED

1.

Under a star a sign fades, loom
detached from fingers, sloped wood
of the golden harp
warped, wing peeled
back into the escarpment, habitat of the newly
slain. Whose name is written? Who
claims passage from bed to bed,
distance folded into sheets
onto which a signature once formed, a shade
once passed, blood ran dry. So a figure
might come out of the distance
into the foreground, carrying flowers
to present at the door, and begin
a nearness, scented, unique.
Then, later, the figure walks over
the hill or down to the corner, turns
into a crowded street, filmic, disappeared.

2.

And now we shall enter the chamber they have
prepared for us, among schoolchildren,
their toy bears and books, torn and marked in places
by other schoolchildren elsewhere. The conditions
are uneasy, not exactly squalid, verging

onto the discolored passage
from there to here,
rocking slowly as on a boat idling offshore
on a windless day. The seabirds are
aswarm, circling and crying, anticipating
a storm. The day is chilly for June.
A chilly June day.

3.

You are invited to see the assembly of roses
withered or entangled in the bed. You
might come carrying a manifesto
from an earlier time, when roses
were roses, men were men. Hark!
Watch how the hawk
descends in one fell swoop!
Or how the newly arrived
crosses the grass
and there perishes, as if thrown away.
A chilly June day is cause enough
for these deficits to gather in a bouquet of
margins, graphic images
inscribed on cloth, hung on a wall, skin
pierced with love. Trove of incidents,
scale warped into conduits, carried thither, yon.

4.

Nothing fits today among the orphaned
kids sweltering in tents as the shamed
world turns and blisters and sings.
Look away! Look away! Seek not
a path on these dry fields,
they do not lead to water.
What is the name of that sound?
Something is climbing, or flying, or
crawling across our horizon
dragging a load of used parts
and a handheld tool.
Fools that we are, we sit, waiting
for a saint in his blue robes
to usher us out of here. *Get out of here.*

DIS

Footsteps with a hiss attached, *dis dis dis*, dragging a mutant shadow from which the object has gone.

A pierced envelope, a membrane, has allowed the figure to escape, as a noun from a sentence, a button from a jacket, a person from life.

They spoke about the *disappeared*, I recall this; a fleet of awful bodies under moving tarps, a desert, a prairie, some hole in the gutter, some sewer, some truck running over hard gravel making the sound of teeth on metal skin.

Nothing is going to get me closer because I don't trust you to be on the other side.

The other side of the mandate to get through or across to the other side, as if in the bright air of evening I could sit and disclose the very amplitude and extent of the lost and found in a flirtatious swell of stories, as if these might deliver the precision for which you have asked but which you have in no way earned.

No, I am not going to abandon the mute, as abhorrent and aberrant as it is, its intact pretense smiling back at you.

If only I could sing.

If I could sing then my body would escape into the pool of notes which might then arrange themselves as a soul, it has been done, I have heard these transformations as I know you have, when whatever we imagine has been seen has then been forfeited, excluded, thrown, its bloods released into poppies and sunsets, so that pathos, the tears of Mary, the tears of a girl, these are strewn into the receptive air, without echo or retrieval, no ghost, no dream recalled; a chord from which the singer can drag a lament, nothing to do with melody, nothing to do with pleasure.

This is why I listen to the cello suites over and over, as they seem to exist above the breach and to travel alongside, as fluid companions to the dissonant assembly below.

If you are awaiting the figure, it will not emerge.

The image is bare, which is why I must forsake it, to protect it from the cruelty of the emulating shadow with its arrogant intimacy, its false embrace in the flare of lit space: candles, dawn, that slit of moon.

Dangerous and sly, unable to form the slightest attachment, the merest touch with its object, it caresses the night with an affinity so entire it cannot be discerned.

You see, don't you, how appearance is a form of betrayal.

ON RELATION

After a while, you run out of news and so words decline.
The better way would be not to worry about your news

or even the news. Words don't care about your or the
news. Words are indifferent to how you are feeling about

your feelings; they do not care if you see something or
say something. Words congregate among themselves

and are safe from your gestures, your desire
to have them meet you exactly where or as meaning

is. If you would look around, you would see
that words do not wish or care to be included

in your pursuit of the right, the perfect, the one.
They need not attach themselves to that this or this that.

HEARSAY

What did you say I said? What? And in that dream
I was married to her, and she—

I don't know who she was, perhaps she was you,
perhaps only me marrying a better me,

perhaps now drilling down into its absurdity
like a mole in the grass whose head got bit off by my cat

before it was a metaphor. *Like* or *as*? I always forget.
It is too hot and the garden is sad, moving to its final stage,

never a pretty sight. I, too, am moving to my final stage.
Stage is also an interesting word, as we think perhaps

of Marlene Dietrich or Lena Horne or
Prince, they, then, I danced to, with my then bf,

in Minneapolis. O Minneapolis! What did? What did they
say he said? The garden is sad. It is too hot. The trouble with

doing things on a hope and some words is they don't always
come true. *All men are created equal.* All

that talking the talk, saying the said. What did he say
I said? And after the final stage? When one has walked

or been dragged off, so the whole scene is as empty as
the glass by my bedside. The glasses by my father's bed-

side were kept separate while he, while we were quarantined
for polio, which killed him, and then I would try to find him

in a dream. Word was that Marlene Dietrich made a pass
at him, and I have a gold-plated knife he stole from the

embassy in Moscow. Someone used the knife to pry
something open, so it is damaged at its point,

the way things get damaged by ill use. Do words
get damaged by ill use? Scratched, torn, stained,

dulled down to their thinnest shadow, the shadow of
lies and cruelty, as when you wandered out of earshot.

COMPANY

Take me with you. These were already worn, these gloves.
I prefer the question previously raised, in that other year
among strangers. Quicksand and strangers. And
the aesthetic questions? Ignore them, they
are old, they are dust. The moon, also, dust
from time to time illumined with a bright wish. Ignore it.
I might ask to be released from turbulence
if only you would forgive whatever sin I committed, as
if in sleep, striking with my glass sword the fixed mountain
with its false gold sunset, peeling the glue from my fingers,
sleeping in my sweater. The dawn begs: do not wake up.
Why stampede when the ghost of Anne Hutchinson
is shivering in the snow, still whispering, *I desire*
to know wherefore I am banished.
Works, grace, footprints,
the wet alignment of dream sex, somewhat resembling.
Lovers, their postcards, meetings under the eaves
all the long summer days.
Look aside, forgive me, step across the boundary
where a rude addendum is carved into urban stone.
They went from pause to glittery pause, carrying
boxes made from bark torn from dead
ash trees. The bricks were darkly stained, as if they had
wept oil, the oil massed, distributed, like a thick
emptiness. Take me with you. I have lost sight of the girl
holding a bag filled with constellations

yet to be drawn. Did you follow her?
Where to? The numbered cards
were all the same suit, red and black, one to ten,
their small nouns stacked, like memories, into order.
She awaits the Fool, his slain pet, his hungry eye,
one way to pass the time in winter;
the Magician, from an earlier game, long since gone.
You see how one dawdles
when information is scarce? You see how the glass
is marred with fingerprints? They were already used,
those gloves.

      The necessary foils a curtailed
agenda, blown out so we faced the dark
blissful and ordinary as clouds
arranged as bodiless wings. Quickly, quickly,
metamorphosis happens, and a radiance
burns through, despite adhesions, despite
the familiar stench lingering in history.
Under this alphabet there is another, recessed,
entangled, its charge curved into
rings of hair, rings of bone, its
vocabulary remote.
Learn again to speak.
The observed world—
iterations, images, stories,
ceaseless pictorial stunts
masquerading as language—
turns from sight, even

as the bird feeder lies on the ground and warm air
pulses thin paper like disturbances
among the departed: Leslie in claret velvet
smiling; Joe holding a glass, shirt open, so
pleased to be Joe; Stacy standing with Chet
by the window on Duane Street, her face
half lit; John speaking from his long shelf, mildly,
ever kind in the cruel regime of the perpetually cruel.
They, there: the unapproachable crowd's molecular dust.

She copied the assignment down, word for word.
She made a list, hoping to loosen its grip
on the foliage. She changed her mask;
she wiped the breath from her glasses
thinking of Celan and of Arendt; thinking mostly
of Blake. A gang of white boys, smoking, assembled
at the corner in their tight shirts and jeans, their
polished hair. And Louise? Her unborn
wrapped in burlap and hung from the ceiling,
like huge wasp nests. The hemlock, also,
wrapped against deer for the winter. The mother,
bleeding, clutched half a strand of pearls. The rest
returned to the sea, over which fireworks cascaded
upward, meticulous as spiderwebs.
What, she wondered, is precious? *Let us try for once,*
Kentridge had said from the library stage: *the cost of change*
disappears, he added. Where? Into the momentum
of immaterial delirium, hidden beneath the salty waves

to mingle with the accumulated tears shed

for the newly dead.

On the round table, a pinkish glass bowl filled

with dry magnolia leaves. She wished

not to look back. She wished to stay,

to believe she might go on ahead. *Now, as always, it*

is early; it is dawn.

Take me with you, into the day. Let me

carry your tools, let me help you over the stream.

Intent's discrepancy performs its sabotage.

She vowed to show up

but now, as always, it is too late, the day

half gone into blank,

the man unknown, his hand on her breast,

perhaps a doctor; perhaps someone's

brother, or father, or son. Who would mend

the basket? Who sew the hem? Who

lift the bleeding boy up off the street?

What economy caused

this, what threshold

crossed, skirt muddy, hands

swollen with tasks an ancient song had preached?

Christmas Eve I announced I wanted

to have a conversation about materialism.

There had been no gifts. Everyone was lonely

and bereft. Everyone, no exceptions, not

even the beloved. The remark fell into
the stormy night like a shooting star, invisible,
so no one made a wish. No one said, *What?*
Remember when the ferry pulled away
from shore, and the receding land
seemed increasingly phantom as it flattened,
a silhouette against the horizon, like
Catalina Island behind this poem on the screen?
It was that kind of moment: arrested distant
silence. The reverie faded, too, with its ribbons
and bulbs, tinsel twisting in the breeze,
the kids on the bed with their stockings,
walnuts and mandarins and balls wrapped
with surprises. *What did you get?*
A frog and a bell and a green plastic ring.

You failed, hissed the Fool from his stool in the closet.
You failed the test, and you can't do it over.
As if there were a story. As if it could be told
and told again without variant, not a single word
out of place, like a ballad sung generation to generation,
carrying its sentiments forward on its old tune.
Repeat after me, O O O. The song always begins with an O.
The Os are behind me now, obedient as pets.
The Fool isn't talking to me, he is talking to you.

A SUPPLICATION

Cold docile triumph   word bank   sell this fund
buy infrastructure   before war
before collapse contaminates the real thing the real
harbor   set sail   set margins   set the game
of tried vocabularies   trusting
their anomalies &

                  speak to us, please,
be present, be among those
who come forward wearing thin armor   carrying
baskets. Say hello, be gentle and fierce.
Do not fear the past. Bring candor, humor, touch.

THE BLUE DOOR

1.

The obligatory cancels its strophe. Let me get a grip,
and begin in this other patch where the air is.

Am I among the vanishing? How does it feel?
As if turning, as if falling, as if coming

unstuck from the body's inconvenience?
Too many questions spoil the poem.

The poem-as-poem cannot reply.
Which is why we need more voices, even

as we know what happens when
there are more voices. Noise, argument, rupture.

Why not a single voice, one that
represents everyone? Poem? Are you listening?

A crucible of dalliance supersedes Goldilocks
and all other pending catastrophes

angling toward power. As if on the last
day you could recall power.

If only the field could retract
into a new beginning, intact, complex,

the geography of the many
seeding the plural world with accord,

good replicating good; evil,
singular, kept to its barren agenda.

Prayers and wishes could then speed
our recovery from the uninhabitable

scald of the venal market.
Not to be hysterical or polemical. Not to

confuse personal anxiety with the future.
I was once at the Stray Dog Cabaret, once in

unlit neighborhoods where sexy initiatives
were underway, awaiting Jim Jarmusch.

Clubs, bars, sudden upswept encounters
with the privileged poor. Dancing with the stars.

Meanwhile.

Meanwhile, another beginning in another district.
I am seeing the headlights of an oncoming

vehicle; I am seeing filmic snow.
O, and I am stepping into the new day

like a doe among bucks, a girl in sequins.
I am trying not to count lovers, or shoes.

The shoes
gather, episodic, in twos.

There are no agents,
no inscriptions,

as the story flows down into a rescinded pile.
I have come to fear the punctuated day.

I have come to wish I had done things differently,
never to have begun with such sad disclosures.

Absent the stanza, the difficult vocabulary,
wandering barefoot along an avenue,

before these piles, these sticks,
the distant lump of dark vestigial matter

and skittering sounds from under the floor
lasting until dawn, and so

looking outward, where skies assemble
their beautiful reconnaissance

traveling, as if beckoning, as if to include.

2.

There are countless children wandering.

Singles and plurals, one shoe, many children

or one child, many shoes. These

discrepancies confuse the grammatical

police; they do not know what to arrest.

Please speak carefully, as this is a vote,

and whether or not you have shoes

you need to say, to choose

whether or not. What undergirds

these words? What might be found?

A frugal sandal or the dazzling

technicolor magic

of the good witch's

rubies? Everyone is after ruby slippers.

We might sort through the archive of sneakers,

the branded stores; we might look

at the feet of strangers, shod in tar and

mildew, mud and blood, the goo

trammeled underfoot, like history.

The southern sky has turned peachy.
I would like to wear it out tomorrow
as a slip. And so slip
through the hole in the sky
into the azure assembly, the tiered swerve
from universe to universe, in my new attire
looking for a mate, or moonstruck
in the glitter of heaven. No guns allowed.
If you listen carefully, you can hear the thrum
of insomniac wings pulsating between episodes of cloud.
In this atmosphere, nothing is shut,
and so motion is the rule, motion without time,
this time, our time, our habit of counting up
and counting down, speaking in numbers
as if they were thought. In the distance I hear
the sound of a creature being slain by another
creature. *The beings I love are creatures.*

Is writing a way of stalling for time,
to delay the tasks in the next room,
dishes and clothes, books and papers,
the pile of shoes on the floor, the floor,
the rugs, the drawer

chaotic with nails and hooks and small tools?

Poem is too busy to answer.

Words are like small magnets,

pulling other words toward them, one by one,

so the singles gather and as they gather

they attest to an alignment that will become

meaning. What was it you said about naming?

It makes a way between unbeing and being,

the definite flowing into the circulating infinite,

the blue door opening the night sky.

in memory: Kenward Elsmlie

NOCTURNE

It turns out there wasn't a door, so she stood looking at the wall, and then at the ground, and then again at the wall, and then up at the sky. The sky was doorless, which was comforting, especially at night, when she could make images from the stars by drawing lines between and among them, as the earliest persons had done as they walked along on the desert sand. But now, looking up into the brightly strewn array, she could not draw a door because the shapes she saw resembled other geometries and, although everything seemed infinitely open, there was no way through. Perhaps, she thought, I can draw something else, not a door, but simply a path; why would anyone want to be inside when the way through cannot be enclosed. Why am I sad that there is no door? she asked herself, and then she saw how she had turned in the night air, and found herself entirely enclosed. And she asked herself, How is it possible to be at once enclosed and illuminated.

DOOR

Small incident last among closings
a singular display confirmed

not the risky allowance of fate not
accruing slowly as in a habit

certainly not mere weather not
choosing a hinge or a lock

entity spreading outward voracious as oil
the collapsed wings trapped

a condition and its picture
what was once shuttered

allowing light in   allowing the moment
to resist passage yes

that endowment   the image
simple recursive

darkly enfolded—
ancient as night   traversing loss

and the abrasion
an appeal   to be   restored.

Acknowledgments

Paul Slovak has kept a room for poetry in the megaverse of corporate publishing. My continued, deepest gratitude to him for seeing my last six collections into print, always with patience, kindness, and receptive attention. One could do no better than Paul for an editor.

In America, poetry is a cottage industry: intimate in scale, amateur in status. Its focus is close-up but not exclusionary; it wants to connect persons to words so to make the world more vivid, life more engaged, between and among us. In my cottage, colleagues and students at Bard College, and friends beyond, have joined in an animated and animating conversation, despite the treacherous conditions we are living through; their commitment to an assembly of active thought has been sustaining and comforting. Among them, Thomas Wild, Michael Ives, Marina van Zuylen, Dinaw Mengestu, Daniel Mendelsohn, Celia Bland, Michael Brenson, Carla Harryman, Nancy Shaver, Roberto Tejada, Kit White, Andrea Barnet, Sterrett Smith, David Levi Strauss, Dan Beachy-Quick, Lisa Pearson, and Richard Kraft: ongoing thanks for, and pleasure in, your company.

To students: thank you for your presence in our exchanges; be vigilant, don't settle, care for words; hold onto your hope, your attention, your humor.

Some of these poems have been previously published, often in earlier drafts. I am grateful to the editors at *The Brooklyn Rail*, *Conjunctions*, *Harper's Magazine*, *HERE*, and *The New York Review of Books*. Most especially, to Bradford Morrow, the great editor of *Conjunctions*, who has been the most generous supporter of my work for forty years: admiration, thanks, and love.

MARINA VANZUYLEN

Poet and essayist Ann Lauterbach is the author of ten previous books of poetry and three books of essays, including *The Night Sky: Writings on the Poetics of Experience* and *The Given & The Chosen*. Her 2009 collection of poetry, *Or to Begin Again*, was a finalist for the National Book Award. Lauterbach's work has been recognized by fellowships from, among others, the Guggenheim Foundation and the John D. and Catherine T. MacArthur Foundation. She is the Ruth and David Schwab II Professor of Languages and Literatures at Bard College. A native of New York City, she lives in Germantown, New York.

PENGUIN POETS

PHILLIS LEVIN
May Day
Mercury
Mr. Memory & Other Poems

PATRICIA LOCKWOOD
Motherland Fatherland
  Homelandsexuals

WILLIAM LOGAN
Rift of Light

J. MICHAEL MARTINEZ
Museum of the Americas

ADRIAN MATEJKA
The Big Smoke
Map to the Stars
Mixology
Somebody Else Sold the World

MICHAEL MCCLURE
Huge Dreams: San Francisco
  and Beat Poems

ROSE MCLARNEY
Forage
Its Day Being Gone

DAVID MELTZER
David's Copy: The Selected
  Poems of David Meltzer

TERESA K. MILLER
Borderline Fortune

ROBERT MORGAN
Dark Energy
Terroir

CAROL MUSKE-DUKES
Blue Rose
An Octave Above Thunder:
  New and Selected Poems
Red Trousseau
Twin Cities

ALICE NOTLEY
Certain Magical Acts
Culture of One
The Descent of Alette
Disobedience
For the Ride
In the Pines
Mysteries of Small Houses

WILLIE PERDOMO
The Crazy Bunch
The Essential Hits of Shorty
  Bon Bon

DANIEL POPPICK
Fear of Description

LIA PURPURA
It Shouldn't Have Been
  Beautiful

LAWRENCE RAAB
The History of Forgetting

BARBARA RAS
The Last Skin
One Hidden Stuff

MICHAEL ROBBINS
Alien vs. Predator
The Second Sex
Walkman

PATTIANN ROGERS
Flickering
Generations
Holy Heathen Rhapsody
Quickening Fields
Wayfare

SAM SAX
Madness

ROBYN SCHIFF
A Woman of Property

WILLIAM STOBB
Absentia
Nervous Systems

TRYFON TOLIDES
An Almost Pure Empty
  Walking

VINCENT TORO
Tertulia

PAUL TRAN
All the Flowers Kneeling

SARAH VAP
Viability

ANNE WALDMAN
Gossamurmur
Kill or Cure
Manatee/Humanity
Trickster Feminism

JAMES WELCH
Riding the Earthboy 40

PHILIP WHALEN
Overtime: Selected Poems

PHILLIP B. WILLIAMS
Mutiny

ROBERT WRIGLEY
Anatomy of Melancholy and
  Other Poems
Beautiful Country
Box
Earthly Meditations:
  New and Selected Poems
Lives of the Animals
Reign of Snakes
The True Account of Myself as
  a Bird

MARK YAKICH
The Importance of Peeling
  Potatoes in Ukraine
Spiritual Exercises
Unrelated Individuals Forming
  a Group Waiting to Cross